FEELINGS THOUGHTS AND EMOTIONS

SHAILJA KUMAR

Cyberwit.net
HIG 45 Kaushambi Kunj, Kalindipuram
Allahabad - 211011 (U.P.) India
http://www.cyberwit.net
Tel: +(91) 9415091004
E-mail: info@cyberwit.net

Printed at VCORE CONNECT LLP.

Dedication

I dedicate this book to my father
Prof. N.K Devaraja

To all the intellectuals of this world who
Inspire us to think, create and bring change.
Eckhart Tolle, Neil Donald Walsh, Joe Dispenza
Deepak chopra, Penache, Desai, Joesph Cambell
Don Miquei, Michael Sayer and all the others.
Oprah, who introduced me to so many great mind
On her Super Soul Sunday show

Acknowledgement

I am extremely thankful to Dr. Anuj.

for his support and help to get this book done.

My friend Ericka Bondy Prat for her help

My husband Atul Kumar for his help.

There is a flame burning,
In the depth of my heart,
This is the light of Faith,
Hope and Gratitude
                    Shailja Kumar

Poetry

A poem is a dance of words. The When strong emotions and thoughts ride the words, poetry is born.

The dancer dons the costumes of emotions to perform; with the words and verses.

When the anguished heart aches, when joy and happiness pervade, when sweet sensations of love infiltrate the heart, the laughter, the piercing pain. It's all played out on paper with a pen and ink.

Poetry is the alchemy of thoughts in words. It guides us toward the path to beauty, joy and wisdom. It paves the way for an enriched life. As music heals and comforts aching hearts and souls, poetry brings clarity and sparks of positive energy. It clears up the darkness within and infuses light and brightness to change the perception of our life's direction. It facilitates our thoughts to soar to lofty heights, experience the rainbows that our lives can be - full of wonder and colors - emerging through the dark wet clouds.

My Vision of Life

To live with ease, to breathe freely, I have accumulated insights for the directives of my life, through reading, meditation and assimilation of the words imparted by great intellectuals.

My thoughts, emotions and the principal directives of my life, pave the way for me to express this through my writings.

The wealth I have accumulated from reading the books of great writers, their infinite wisdom is indefinable. It is like finding treasure and joy simultaneously. I attempt to create an insightful enquiry of my intimate thoughts and guiding principles of life through my poems and writings.

Contents

SEGMENT 1

Silence

When a man knows the solitude of silence and feels the joy of quietness, he is then free from fear and sin and he feels the joy of 'Dhamma the eternal law of the Universe

Dhammapada

*Silence in all its glory
manifests wisdom of life
love and spirituality*

Shailja

Silence

Glorious, soundless, colorless abstract,
Contemplative of eternal truth.
Turn on the sound of silence,
The gateway to meditation,
Let its echoes reverberate,
In the dark corridors of mind,
To clear the pathways,
To bring in "Sublime happiness".

As it grows,
Opens up new horizons,
To inspect the self and to explore,
The deep hidden layers of mind,
To unveil the truth;
The truth of life and existence.
It will set your free,
From the shackles of ignorance,
To bring peace, harmony and tranquility.

....

.

Cheers

Dreaming when dawn's left hand was in the sky.
I heard a voice within the tavern city
Awake my little ones and fill the cup
Before life's liquor in its cup be dry

Omar Khayyam

Make of most of what we may still spend before into dust we decend.

Shailja

Cheers

Take a high road to joy,
Make happiness your destination,
Have a stiff drink of love and compassion,
Add a little good will and cheer,
Add some zest to fill up the pitcher,
Now raise the glasses,
With friends and those dear,
Toast your life with good wishes and cheers.

. . . .

Live

Encapsulate the moments of bliss;
In the time you have,
For every fleeting moment brings a change,
Savor it, live it, and drown in it, drink it,
Till time relinquishes it.

SHAILJA

Live

Live life to the fullest;
For it's not here to stay.
Relish and savor each moment,
Garnish with love and joy,
Keep the gloom at bay.
Now don the good motives and ride,
The horse of high hopes.
Let go of constraints,
To venture out into the sphere of life,
Unbound, untethered, like a wild river,
That gathers strength to form,
A beautiful cataract.
Soar up high; in the open skies,
Become a spark of light that glows,
May it even be for a moment or so,
But glow and shine in your light,
Before you diffuse forever.
In the dusty brine of confine,
Called death.

. . . .

Mystery of life

Life is a natural unfolding of happenings.
Michael Saylor

When you remove the negative elements of your thoughts and actions - you clear the path for the flow of positive energy that ignites and lights up your mind to a higher level of consciousness that connects you with the divine.
SHAILJA

Mystery of Life

The mystery of life;
Who can unfold its secrets.
The mystery of universe;
Its fury and blessings.
No roads are paved to reach our destinations,
Only paths leading to the unknown.
We delight in unwrapping gifts,
Not knowing what wonder or joy it holds,
Such is life, wrapped in mystery.
When pathway and doors appear,
Don't let the opportune moment go unveil,
For the fear of the unknown.
How to tread these paths,
how to get through doorways!
It's entirely up to you.
You get to choose the right from wrong,
Don't let the efforts be a waste in haste,
Just follow the clues from your head and heart.
For therein lies the key to unlock,
the potential; to grant joy, peace and love,
To lead you to your destination.

．．．．．．．．．．．．．．．．．．．．．．．．．．．．．．

Mute Melodies

Evil is the absence of light, of love.
Gary Zukav

Mute Melodies

When day dissolves;
Dark, obscure forms dance around,
Strike darkness with mute melodies,
Releasing desires, confined and encapsulated.
In the dark layers of mind,
The greed and agony of these desires,
Rupture the delicate fibers of the sensitive core.
It's shattered fragments fly around,
To be devoured by ghostly shadows,
And the break of dawn becomes,
A vision of renewed hope.

. . . .

Despair

"I wish I could show you when you are lonely in the darkness, the astonishing light of your own being"

Hafiz

Despair

Do not despair my aching heart,
"I am here to hold your sorrows"
The tears may roll in agony,
As you may yearn for blithe tomorrows.
Let loose those tears to flow,
To cleanse and rid the sorrows.

Only you can feel the joyous beat,
Or the rhythm of pulsating grief.
When dreams wither like autumn leaves,
Hold back the tears and angst,
Envision a sparkling day after,
In the infinite field of possibility.

It's just you and me my aching heart.
It's up to us to dissolve the pain,
The band keeps playing the song of life,
Don't skip the beat just join the game.
Time rolls to move forward,
It's up to you to keep going.

. . . .

Change of season

The flower that smiles today, tomorrow dies.
All that we wish to stay
Tempts and then flies.
What is the world's delight?
Lightening that mocks the night
Brief even as bright.

P.S. Shelly

Change of Seasons

A sigh of joy; to a sigh of woe.
The path dwindles,
From open vistas to confined sphere.
O life! O sweet sufferings of the soul.
The body decays, the mind seeks console.
Memories are folded neat and compressed,
To be buried deep and put to rest.
To be a spectator, is all we ask,
To borrow mirth; to fill our flask.
The warmth of love once willingly shared,
Is ours to seek; to fill the hearth.

. . . .

A walk in the woods

Sorrow is hushed into peace in my heart like the evening among trees.

Rabindranath Tagore

A Walk in The Woods

A walk in the woods to cleanse the mind,
The whispers of the swaying pines,
Soft rustling of the dancing leaves,
And the whistling of melodious breeze.
Soars my spirit to the realm of your love.

The gentle kindness of the benevolent sky,
Outshines the worldly blithe.
The gentle lapping of the waves ashore,
The echoes of sea mariner's lore,
Enchants the soul to a soft lull

The light and warmth of the golden sun.
The fragrant meadows;
The blooming fields;
Cast a spell of rapture in our senses
With beauty unbound and divine.

Moonlight

She walks into beauty, like the moon on the starry night.

J. Keats

Beauty thou art a wonderer on the earth.
And has no temple in the isle.
In more than one sweet dialect
thou hast spoken.

Walter Savage Landos

She was a Phantom of delight.
When she first gleamed upon my sight,
A lovely Apparition, sent.
To be a moments' ornament.

W. Wordsworth

Moonlight

The moon ascends the sky.
The moonlight descends on earth,
In it's silvery splendor,
She glides in her elegance.
The Goddess of the night,
Spreading beauty and grandeur.
A feast to the eyes,
An opiate for the senses.
Accompanied with the stars,
She spreads rapture of love,
Creating; mystical, magical aura,
To weave dreams,
To sparkle the minds with joy and hope,
And to ignite passions of the heart,
This is moonlight,
the lady of the night.

....

The Journey

The existence of ours is as transient as autumn clouds.
To watch the birth and death of beings is like looking at the
movements of a dance.
A lifetime is like a flash of lightening in the sky.
Rushing by like a torrent down a steep mountain.

Buddha

Move into the realm of manifestation
When you are one with the present - the divine - you are here
to consciously allow the unfolding.

Michail Bernard Bekwitch

Our birth is but a sleep and forgetting.
The soul that rises with our own life's star,
Hath had elsewhere its setting.

William Wordsworth

The Journey

I walked a walk of thousand miles,
To reach the destination of my life.
The miles stretched; as I went on;
To the far end of endless time.
No sign of destination in sight,
Although I walked a thousand miles.

Over the hills and in meadows,
The grasslands and prairie shadows,
The deep rivers I swam,
Under the ocean currents I sank,
Over the mountain tops I climbed,
Through the dusty paths to find.

I walked a walk of a thousand score,
And gently filled the track afore.
In the remnant shadows of my thoughts,
Nowhere to run; nowhere to walk,
No clue to where my destination was,
I sat defeated and lost.

A stranger then crossed my path,
He said, "my friend you look lost".
Prepare yourself for the journey of life,
Discard the things, to you that surround,
Seek beyond the mundane sphere of life,
Direct your search to your heart and mind.

I walked all night and in the dark shadows saw a light.
There sat a saint with a smile so faint,
The rays of light danced around him in glee.
He gestured me to sit on the ground,
With crossed legs and folded hands afore,
I closed my eyes as if in prayer, freed my mind of every care.

With closed eyes; I walked all night
In my dreams; I saw a sight.
A grove of trees that bore no leaves,
No flowers nor any fruit,
Just bare branches held high towards the sky,
To thank for joyous gift of life.

No tender flowers graced to bloom,
No chirping birds, no nesting eggs,
No butterflies dancing around in loops,
No ripe fruit to be plucked to consume,
The fruit was attached to the root,
Under the layers of dirt and rocks.

In the morning light I saw a sight,
Ten thousand birds suspended up in air.
Chirping and fluttering without a care,
No grove of trees to rest their feet,
They danced and pranced to life's melodies,
They hung in air without a care.

I walked and walked with all my might,
Lo and behold! witnessed a sight,
The sky hung high, the earth sunk low,
There I was - amidst of it all,
Suspended in midair without a woe,
No bumps, no knocks, no earthly foes.

. . . .

The road was there, but it was bare,
Chards of broken glass littered everywhere,
The sand glistened in the burnished heat,
The water in the lakes stood still; so very still.
No fish moved to take a swim,
There was no wind; the world was still.

I closed my eyes, the time stood still,
So tranquil and so peaceful.
In the stillness flashed a light,
Soothing and so very bright.
In the midst of all, echoed a voice,
This is the destination of your life.

I closed my eyes to hear some more,
No laden thoughts of mortal woes,
A simple path for you to go.
Let ordinary treasures be embraced.
May the life with health, love and joy be enriched.
The journey we seek; is: the one within.

Mother

"We are born of love: Love is our mother"
                                        Rumi

Mother 1

The truth of you:
The love of you;
Is the life of you.
Fortitude and forbearance,
Is the strength of you.,
Your luminous thoughts and actions,
Is the wealth of you.
Your thoughtfulness, your gentle kindness,
Is the essence of you.
You are timeless,
You are the mother, you are the daughter.
The future of life is you.
Peace, tranquility and love
Is the presence of you.

Mother 2

Your sweet whispers I hear,
When the soft breeze blows.
Your footsteps; ever so gentle,
When thinking of you.
When I am lonely and sad,
When tears struggle to trickle down,
I feel you close to me.
Whispering... things can't be so bad,
For you to part with pearly tears.
Cheer up! sweet child cheer,
You are given so much,
Don't be sad, love, live, be joyful,
This is just a bend, not an end,
It shall pass.
Be thankful for the life you have,
Be grateful for the bounty given,
For you have enough to recharge,
Your life, your future, your destiny,
Just count the blessings not sorrows

House of dreams

There is light in you the world cannot perceive. And with its eyes you will not see this light, for you are blinded by the world. Yet you have the eyes to see it. It is there for you to look upon. This light is the reflection of the thought we practice now. To feel the love of God within you is to see the world anew, shinning in innocence, alive with hope, and blessed with perfect clarity and love.

Lesson 189 A Course In Miracles.

"Dreams are a royal road to happiness" Sigmund Freud

House of Dreams

The million dreams we dream,
In the shadows of night,
Vanish at day break.
The dreams wait night after night,
Hidden in the midst of darkness;
Waiting to be awakened.
The love we crave flourishes,
In the hidden layers of obscurity,
Like a flicker of light.
Dreams carry us to wondrous magical path.
A path; that doesn't stretch far.
The solitary moon sheds light.
On a haunted, dilapidated house.
To awaken us from the myth.
The myth of dark love,
And the house of dreams.

. . . .

Smile

Can death be sleep, when life is but a dream.
And scenes of bliss pass as a phantom by.
The transient pleasures as a vision
And yet we think the greatest pains to die.
> *Keats*

Water never forgets that the sea is its destiny and that sooner
or later it must be reached.
> *Paulo Coelho*

Smile

When I am feeble and old
Just smile at me.
When life exhausts me,
When the mirror mocks me,
Just smile at me.

When these legs fail to carry
The body so frail,
When these arms no longer reach,
To hug or embrace,
Just hug and smile at me.

When the ears stop listening,
To the joyous melodies of life,
When tears reveal,
The sadness of life,
Just smile at me.

When the body gives up,
It shudders and crashes to a heap.
Let me sleep in the deep.
Most peaceful sleep,
and smile for me.

. . . .

Tears

A single act of kindness throws out roots in all directions.
And the roots spring up and make new trees.
                                    Amelia Earhart

This is my Wish for you.
Comfort on difficult days,
Smiles, when sadness intrude,
Rainbows to follow the clouds,
Laughter to warm your heart
Hugs when spirit sag.
        *

                        Ralph Waldo Emerson

Tears

For all the desolate and broken,
For their shattered hopes and dreams,
For lives impacted by misfortunes,
I shed tears.
When sky shoots arrows of thunderous rain,
When earth splits to devour its children,
When mountains spew the molten rocks,
I shed tears.
When hunger pangs make children wail,
When mother's love does not sustain,
For little souls who lived in vain,
I shed tears.
For all the wanderers of wrong tracks,
Who bear the consequence it begets,
For their suffering and grief.
I shed tears.
For the ones unloved, uncared for,
Treated unkind; yet gave their all,
The unfortunate and the lonely lot,
I shed tears.
Those who died while still living,
Craved compassion in their afflictions,
Lying under the mounds of dirt,
Un-mourned and forgotten;
I say a prayer for them.

....

Confrontation

Few people are capable of expressing with equanimity opinions which differ from prejudices of their social environment. Most people are even incapable of forming such opinions.

Albert Einstein

If you are always trying to be normal you will never know how amazing you can be.

Maya Angelou

Confrontation

Confronted with,
The bare reality of life,
My identity drowns, dissolves,
In agony of abysmal thoughts.
The flaky concepts, the fabricated truth;
Of our existence,
Created to mask the ignorance,
Of the feeble minds.

In this chaos; I search for,
The spontaneous truth.
The revelations of untainted minds,
To cleanse the falsified grime,
To reveal the essence of our true existence,
Like distilled raindrops,
Making its way to the earth,
Through the dark massive clouds.

. . . .

Cup of tea

Some day. some day
O troubled breast

Shalt thou find rest.

W. Wordsworth

And you will accept the seasons of your heart, even as you have always accepted the seasons that pass over your fields.

Kahil Gibran

Cup of Tea

Cold, cloudy day,
Gale trapped among the trees,
Shuddering, agitating and howling,
Many a whispering; circulating,
In the wind.
Reviving the memory of dear ones;
 Departed and long gone
The pain hits like a tidal wave,
Water streaming down my face.
A cup of warmth,
Borrowed from tea cup pressing my palms.
The fingers lace around the heat.
To relieve the pain.

....

Obscure journey

Can death be sleep, when life is but a dream.
And scenes of bliss pass as a phantom by the transient
pleasures as a vision seem.
And yet we think the greatest pain's to die.

Keats

Obscure Journey

Where do people go;
When they leave the earthly abode,
The vast blue sky looks down;
At the wiped existence,
The imprints of human footsteps recede
Memories hang in the air a while,
Then blown away into oblivion

…………………………..

Death of love

If everything around you looks dark,
Look again, you may be the light.
                                    Rumi

Seek not outside yourself for it will fail
and you will weep each time an idol falls
Heaven cannot be found where it is not.
                          A course in miracles.

Death of Love

As love dies;
A slow and silent death,
The tears dry out.
The heart is ripped and torn apart.
And we silently watch just watch,
The pieces fall one after the other,
Disintegrate into nothingness.
No screams are heard,
No tears wiped,
Just the deafening calm;
Of the deathly silence,
Pervades over the senses,
To haunt your empty heart,
With silent screams.

. . . .

Hope

Believe you can and you're halfway there.
                    T. Roosevelt

Success is not final.
Failure is not fatal.
It is the courage to continue that counts.

Hope

The audacity of hope; can be found.
In the darkest regions of our hearts and minds.
The resilience of human spirit,
Let mankind survive and thrive.
The dogged perseverance; help face;
The evasive times,
Encourage us to emerge anew,
Whole, and unscathed,
To seize and eradicate our fears,
The fear of living to the fullest,
With zest and enthusiasm.
To strengthen our resolve,
To move forward.

....

Time

Fragile, unpredictable,
Changes its color like a chameleon,
From comforting warmth to stone cold.
It comes and stealthily goes,
No one knows,
When the wind of change blows,
Where the time will command us to go.

………………………..

SEGMENT II

Life

The word encompasses many facets - both painful and pleasant. The high and lows of emotional roller coaster, the encounters of exquisite beauty and joy. On the other hand; numerous unpleasant and hurtful moments transpired by the associations of mean and vicious people. They cause immense pain and scar our lives with their toxic actions; to feed the darkness inherent in their lives.

It is up to us to change the perspective of our lives with pleasant thoughts, good deeds and actions. Negative elements are all around us, so are the positive ones. Negate the negatives and go forward. Pain, fear, evil and hatred, it's around us, so is love, generosity, compassion, joy and hope. The choice is ample - pick the right attributes.

I think of life as a prayer, live it with reverence. Any thought birthing in mind should be nurtured with purity and clarity of good intent.

Every action we take, should benefit others also besides oneself. Every deed should be performed with joy. When we revere everyday events and happenings, when we do not question the outcome of our actions and duties , peace descends on us, and life becomes a prayer. When we choose this path in our life - a myriad of pathways appear that lead us to a peaceful and content life.

"The highest thought is always that thought which contains joy. The clearest words are those when contain truth. The grandest feeling is that feeling which you call love." Neil Donald Walsh

"Karma is the external assertion of human freedom. Our thoughts, our words and deeds are the thread of the net which we throw around ourselves." VIVEKANANDA

What Is Life

As long as you are breathing, there is more right with you than wrong.

The key to happiness is in your power to do so.
Dr. Christian Northope

What is Life

Life is ecstasy and agony,
Blythe and sorrowful,
Lovable, desirable,
Sweet, savory and bitter.
Mysterious!
Complicated,
Unpredictable.
Life is transitory,
Topsy-turvy,
Torrid and bleak,
Joyful!
Comprehend it.
Taste it
Relish it.
Love it.

....

Cup of life

And in the sweetness of friendship
Let there be laughter and sharing of pleasures.
For in the dew of little things the heart finds its morning and
is refreshed.

Kahil Gibran

Cup of Life

Don't carry an empty cup,
Fill it up with life's sweet nectar.
The nectar of love and compassion,
The nectar of gratitude,
Sweeten the life of you and others.
By sharing your warmth;
To release their pain.
Together; you celebrate with joy,
Share hope for bright new tomorrows.
Together you share laughter,
And bury the sorrows.

. . . .

Enrich life

Watch your thoughts, they become words; watch your words, they become actions, they become habits; watch your habits, they become your character, for it becomes your destiny.
Frank Outlaw

When we harness the forces of harmony, joy and love, we create success and good fortune with effortless ease.
Deepak Chopra

Enrich Life

Make your life a prayer.
Blend it with the positives.
Enrich yourself with jewels,
Too precious to be stolen.
Bring reverence to;
Every thought, every act, and deed,
that you deem fit to act upon,
To lead you on the path,
Of peace and contentment.
Live life, to the brim of ecstasy,
For it is not here to stay.
Relish each moment,
Savor love and joy,
Keep the gloom at bay.
Be Grateful;
For all the grandeur life grants
Now gallop on horse called High Hope,
And ride into the sphere called Life.

. . . .

Life Rolls

Life is a natural unfolding of happenings.
Michael Sayer

Heaven is of your own making on earth or in heaven.
Michael Sayer

Life Rolls

Pebbles and gold;
Life rolls.
Silver and tears;
Have no fear.
Drums beat;
So do our hearts.
Birds soar up in the sky,
So do our dreams.
Stars hang up at lofty height;
So do our aspirations.
The moon displays silvery splendor,
Like the moment of wonder.
The sun creates and destructs;
Like our ambitious actions,
Facilitate and impede success.
The soft caressing breeze turns into storms.
The serene rain drops bring joy.
 The thunderous rain causes fear and destruction.
Such is the wheel of life,
It brings high hopes and disappointment,
Creates illusions of thrill and disenchantment,
But life; rolls on.

. . . .

The rainbow of Humanity

Life is given to us, we earn it by giving.
Tagore

The Rainbow of Humanity

Let life unfold its wonder every step of the way,
Let the fire of life illuminate each day.
Let every thought ignite a positive spark,
Let every dream find its way,
Let every step lead to the destiny that awaits.
May every action; every deed paves the way,
For a kinder world; where love abides,
Where generosity resides and mankind thrives.
Let the words and dialogues shared,
Transpire peace, harmony and love.
May every action bring fresh perspective,
For the winds of change.
Change; that breaks the barriers of discrimination and hate.
Change: to make the world safe for human race.
Let us create a rainbow of every ethnic color,
Every caste, and creed for people of this world.
To live under the radiance of,
"The Rainbow of Humanity"

. . . .

Living life

*"Every tragic experience is a getaway to learning.
Listen to the silence of your heart to negate the fear, you are
facing.
Close your eyes, steer your vision inward
find the spark of light, glowing, connecting you to the spirit
in residence."*

Shailja

Karma is both action and the consequence of that action.

Vivekanand

Living Life

The agony and ecstasy of living,
The beauty and joy of shared moments,
The heartache of lost love,
The silence of the broken heart,
The dented spirit of fractured life.
The solace found in prayers,
The abundance of strength in our resolve,
To propel life forward step by step.
The silence of time that heals.
The resilience of human spirit,
Releases the grief.
With a resolve to bury old woes,
The stagnant tears,
Roll down drop by drop,
As fresh new hope knocks and awakens life
To a new dawn.

....

Let it matter

Reverence is an attitude of honoring life. Your intention and attention shape your experiences.
                    Gary K. Zukav

Bring reverence to every aspect of your life, then you will connect with the divine.

What could be more powerful than growing to be worthy of yourself.
                    Shailja

Let it Matter

As we live and breathe,
Let every breath matter.
As we walk and move,
Let every step matter.
Every wish that comes true,
Every blessing granted,
let gratitude matter.
Let every thought and dream,
Every action and deed matter.
Let the right direction matter.
Let joy and life matter,
Let it all matter.

....

The ups and downs

Find the place in your heart where there is joy, and the joy will burn
the pain.

Joseph Campbell

Underneath the layers of turmoil in your mind lies the calm.
Zon Kabat Zinn

The Ups and Downs

This is life, filled with love and despair.
It ignites high hopes for wondrous tomorrows,
It inflicts pain and sorrow.
It propels us to the height of ecstasy,
And roll us down in gloom and agony.
Life is a high and low road to extremity.
No matter how high are 'Highs',
How low the 'Lows',
This is the life we are given,
Live with care and understanding,
For life is beyond comprehending.

. . . .

Life's facets

Life is like a prism, multifaceted. To embrace life is to live through all its colors and dimensions.
                                        Shailja

Life is a gift, wrap it with mirth, laughter and love.
                                        Shailja

Life's Facets

Life is a walk of dreamland and wasteland,
It's the softness of flowers and prick of thorns.
Beautiful Spring weather and thunderous storms.
There are nightmares and screams,
There is fulfillment of dreams,
Haunted nights followed by dawns bright,
Amidst your fears and life gone wrong,
Birds chirping melodious songs.
There are roses and chilled champagne,
Shards of broken hearts and promises forgotten.
Life is a vision of hope and fulfillment,
Bouts of despair and discontentment.
It is an uneven landscape and misplaced instances,
You are the landscaper, cultivate the positives everywhere,
Infuse each moment with kind thoughts and deeds.
Then take gentle strides towards your beautiful dream.
On the carpet of life that you weave,
Every loop richly infused with enthusiasm and hope.

. . . .

SEGMENT III

Prayers

Prayer is a conversation with the highest. Prayer is having faith in the power of asking and also receiving. Ask with belief, receive, and be thankful.

"There is a flame burning in the depths of my heart that burns the negativity and paves the way for the flow of positives. This is the light of faith, hope and gratitude that illuminates my soul. This light is the constant awareness of the divine presence. This light is the essence of my existence"

Shailja

My prayer

You are what your deep driving desire is
As your desire is, so is your will
As your will is, so is your deed.
As your deed is, so is your destiny.
                    Brehadarany Upanishad

Truth, joy and love. These three are interchangeable as one leads to the other. For truth is the body, and joy is the blood of God who is love.
                    Neal Donald Walsh

....

My Prayer

Deep within the depth of my being,
May I find peace.
May I find strength to brave all storms.
May the seed of hope and love,
Sprout and branch out to others.
Gently and powerfully,
Within the circle of mankind.
May I radiate peace and love.

****

Path

When you walk the path to connect with the divine, when you surrender to the 'supreme being' you are reborn and replenished.

Shailja

Every prayer, every thought, every statement, every feeling is creative, to the degree that it is fervently held as truth, to that degree will it be made manifest in your experience.

Neil Donald Walsh

....

Path

Show me the path that leads to you,
Show me the light that shines on you,
Grant me the wisdom of your words.
Show me the world through your eye,
Guide me to the place where joy and peace abides.
Guide me to the source of love that fulfills.
Lead me O God to the purer, and gentle life.

****

The intervention

Reverence is an attitude of honoring life. Your intention and attention shapes your experiences.

Gary Zukav

When we seek 'Divine' presence in own lives, when we connect with it the positive flow of energy changes the course of life - leading it towards peace and harmony.

Shailja

The Intervention

Welcome! to my humble abode,
Let your thoughts invade my senses,
To retract from all distractions.
The heavy load of life we carry around,
Bantering, torturing, trying to find its way,
Through incessant wanderings of the mind.
The invasion of petty and shallow thoughts,
The battle of desirable and the undesirable,
Combating for existence to add to the misery,
Of life full of pain, ignorance and sorrow,
Where there are no glorious tomorrows.
Life snuffed out of existence,
Bodies infused with pain,
Anxiety laden thoughts,
Robbing off sleep.
So welcome to my life.
Grant me the wisdom of the wise,
To propel life forward,
With grace, dignity and joy.

****

Gems

God is the highest place within you.
An all-encompassing love.
The ever present essence of life
'Super Soul Sunday' Oprah

When we live life with purity and joy, when we do not question the outcome of our actions and duties, peace descends on us and life becomes a prayer.

Shailja

Gems

May we seek the guidance,
To the path you've paved.
Pick the gems of wisdom,
That you've strewn and laid.
May we have the insight,
To pick the brightest of the lot,
Then we can traverse the gentler path,
To bask and shine in faith and trust,
Of your glorious light.

****

Let

When you connect with positive energy and surrender your ego, a luminous path unfolds, that leads to purer forms of life, the life intended to be lived.

Shailja

Let

Let your love and grace shine through me,
May I be the messenger of your thought,
The gospel of your words.,
The hymn to be sung for you,
The sea that parts for you.
The still waters for you to walk on.
May I be the prayer for you,
That thousands say to honor you,
Let this particle of dust be blessed,
To be illumined by you.

. . . .

Gentle rain

Feel the brilliance of energy that created you.
Marriane William

The light shines brightly within us. We choose to both feel it and allow it to continue working as a guiding post or we choose to ignore it to the point of dimming and forget that it even exists.

Sainab Salbi

Gentle Rain

Grant us the gentle rain of love,
To nurture our soul,
Let our thoughts be pure,
Let no evil dare to daunt our soul.
Clear the cobwebs of doubt and fear.
Shine in a "New Light"
Let the harmony of positive thoughts and deeds.
Create a soothing melody,
For life to roll gently,
To steer us to the bright path,
The path that Springs 'New Hope'

. . . .

Divine presence.

*The frail vessel thou emptiest again and again and fillest it
ever with fresh life.
This little flute of a reed thou hast carried over hills and
dales, and hast breathed through it melodies eternally new ...
Thy infinite gifted come to me only on those very small hands
of mine. ... Ages pass and still thou purest and still there is
room to fill.*

Rabindranath Tagore 'Gitanjali'

*How strange it is that man on earth should roam.
And lead a life of woe, but not forsake.
His rugged path; nor dare he view alone
His future doom which is but to awake.*

Keats

....

Divine Presence

Be the light of my life,
The voice of my truth and wisdom
Be the strength to see me through;
The perils of life.
Be the voice of my reasoning.
Constant and persistent.
Through all the seasons of my life.

....

Light and joy

The privilege of life is being who you are. Follow your bliss.
Joseph Campbell

We have within us divine intelligence when you connect to it - you change your life.

Vasistha's Yoga
Swami Venkatesanand

When you move into the realm of manifestation. When you are present with the divine - You are here to consciously allow the unfolding.

Elizabeth Gilbert

Light and Joy

May we walk in light,
May we make the world bright.
Let's dispel the darks,
That tainted our past.
May the road we tread;
Be filled with love and compassion.
May the joy we feel,
Be for giving and sharing.
May our lives be full of hope and cheer,
May we choose laughter over tears.
May the tears that roll down,
To wet our cheeks,
Be of happiness and joy not grief,
May our prayers be for gratitude not need,
May our lives be of peace and content not greed.

. . . .

Guidance

Every action generates force of energy that returns to us in like kind.
What we sow is what w reap.
Deepak Chopra

If we can get out of our own 'self', our yearnings, desires and need and think of others, you will find yourself elevated to a higher level in life and you will find joy.

There is no greater power than to be in harmony with one-self.

Shailja

Guidance

May the path we walk,
Be bright with hope and cheer.
May the love we receive,
Be forwarded to share.
May our trespasses,
Lead us to forgive others.
May we be gentle and kind,
To ourselves and others.
May we learn to be our best,
To give our best to others.
May we learn to unite,
To let world unite together.
In faith, in love and integrity.

....

Light

As impure water poured into pure water becomes one, so also is it with the self of an illumined knows, he becomes one with the supreme.

Upanishads

How far are you from me O fruit?
I am hidden in your heart O flower.

Tagore

Light

You are the light that shines within,
 A thought that dwells hidden,
An emotion that linger,
Buried deep inside my being.
From time to time it needs awakening,
As it settles down dormant and forgotten
Beneath the grind of life.

....

एहसास जज़्बे ख्याल

कविताएं

शेर

शायर का ख्याल इन्सान को जीने की
खूबसूरती देता है

माता–पिता को समर्पित

पिता प्रोफेसर एन.के. देवराजा ने राह दिखायी ज़िंदगी की राह चुनने की एवं माता श्रीमती राजश्वरी ने चिराग जलाये ज्योति और स्नेह के। दोनों के सहयोग से जीवन धारा ढूंढती पहुंची मंज़िल तक......

कुछ शब्द

जिंदगी के कतरों को शब्दों में पिरोया : ज़हन में बसे खूबसूरत लम्हे, कुछ अनदेखे सपने जो अपने बने, ख्यालों के मजमे, जो कागज़ पर उतेर। अनकही, अनसुनी दासतायें, खयाली और बे खयाली की जुर्तें, अधूरे सपने, मुस्कुराहटें, खिली, अधखिली। आहों के भंवर, आंसुओं के सैलाब, अधूरी तमन्नायें और टूटे दिल के बिखरे टुकड़े। इन सबको मिलाकर एक जाम बनाया और कागज़ के टुकड़ों को उसमें डुबोया।

यह कविता संग्रह मेरी ज़िंदगी के आभास है। दुख दर्द की संवेदना, सुख के पलों की रस धारा, ममता के स्त्रोतों की झावट, सकून की बारिष की बौछार, ज़िंदगी की दुत्कारें, वक्त से समझौते और गम के दरिया का बहाव हैं। प्रत्येक व्यक्ति इन तमाम दौरों से गुज़रता जीवन व्यतीत करता है – इसी को जिंदगी कहते हैं। यही मेरे जीवन की भी सच्चाई है।

आप इन रचनाओं को पढ़कर देखें, महसूस करें, शायद इनमें आपको ज़िंदगी का कोई हिस्सा नज़र आये, कुछ चोटें, सुनहरी यादें, खूबसूरत पल जो पुरानी यादों को जाग्रत कर दें। मुमकिन है कि वक्त कुछ देर को वहीं ठहर जाये और आप उसमें खो जायें।

अनुक्रमणिका

"जज़्बे–ए–दिल में खुदा रहता है,
सांसों में उकसा कलमा, आंखों में दीदार का जुनून,
यह ज़िंदगी उसकी अमानत है, हर खुशी उसकी इनायत,
यह दिल उसका दरगा, मेरा मज़हब उसकी इबादत.....

सजदा

उसके नूर से दिन निकला,

उसके ही नूर से चांदनी निखरी,

हवाओं ने उसकी खूशबू बिखराई,

कुदरत ने उसके सजदे की महफिल सजायी,

आंख बंद कर उसकी खुशबू का एहसास कर,

उसके करमों रहम की दाद कर,

यूं तो दिन निकलते हैं और ढल जाते हैं,

हम अपने खयालों के बोझ तले दब जाते हैं,

दो पल को उसकी रहमत का इज़हार कर,

उसके सजदे में सिर झुकाकर शुक्र गुज़ार बन

"तस्वीर तुम्हारे प्यार की दिल पर खिंची है,
खुशबू तुम्हारे इश्क की सांसों में बसी है,
कैसा चैन, कैसा सुकून इस दिल को,
ज़िंदगी की सारी खुशियां तुमसे जुड़ी हैं......"

"खामोश गुलशन को तुम्हारी खुशबू से महकाया है,
हाथ में जाम लेकर, बुझते चिरागों को जलाया है,
तुम्हारी यादों की आतिश को हवा दी,
और इस आग को हमने दिल से सुलगाया है....."

प्यार

एक दिलकश खुशबू, एक खूबसूरत एहसास,

जो हल पल साथ रहता है,

जिसमें जिस्म लिपटा और महकता रहता है,

दिल की गहरायी में ज़िंदा रहने की कशिश,

होंठों पर मुस्कुराहट का सबब,

ज़िंदगी का एक खूबसूरत तोहफा,

कीमती और नायाब,

जो हर किसी को हासिल नहीं होता,

ज़िंदा रहने का मकसद,

जिस मकसद में खुदा रहता है,

यही प्यार होता है.....

"ख्वाबों को पलकों पर सजाकर,
तुम्हारी यादों का दीपक जलाया है,
इस रात को उजाला करने,
फिर तुम्हारा ख्याल आया है....."

खूबसूरत सुबह

आज सुबह उसके चेहरे पर मुस्कुराहट देखी,
लगा जैसे खिली हो गुलाब की कली,
माथे पर बिखरी जुल्फों की लटें,
आंचल में उठती गिरती संतोष की सांसें,
लगा यूं कह रही हों गुज़री रात की कहानी कोई,

कितनी मस्त नींद में सोयी है,
लगता है रंगीन ख्वाबों में सोई है,
चिड़ियों की चहक, सबा की महक,
और सुबह की रौशनी से भी मसरूफ है ये,

बड़ी खुशनसीब है जो बेफिक्र होकर है सोई,
सुबह बयां कर रही घटी जो रात कहानी कोई,
गालों के गुलाब और आंखों के कंवल खिले होंगे,
महुए के जाम भी होंठों से कई बार छलके होंगे,

सोने दो सुकून से इसे कुछ देर और,
रात के नशे को ठहरने दो थोड़ा और,
बड़े नसीब वाली है, किसी के दिल में बसने वाली,
रेशम सी सुहानी महबूबा है, किसी भाग्यवान की,

यह तो प्यार की बारिश में भीगी हुई है,
किसी किस्मत वाले की ज़िंदगी है,
इसे तो प्यार से आशीर्वाद दो,?
लम्बी उम्र और सुखी जीवन की दुआयें दो.....

"तुम गये तो ज़िंदगी गयी,
इन आंखों में, सुनहरे ख्वाबों की सिर्फ तस्वीर रह गयी....."

यही है ज़िन्दगी
ऐ इश्क ऐ ज़िन्दगी
कुछ ग़मज़दा कुछ दिलनशी

यह मदहोश लमहों की रंगीनियां,

यह तन्हा लम्हों की संगीनियां,

किसी दिल में सब्ज−ए−बहार,

तो कहीं, आंसुओं की बौछार,

कुछ तन्हा लम्हों की मजबूरियां,

कुछ जज़्बे दिल की खामोशियां,

कुछ इश्क की मेहरबानियां,

कुछ ख्वाहिशों की नाकामियां,

चंद खुशियों से दिल हुआ गुलजार,

ऐसे दौर से गुज़दी ज़िंदगी बार−बार,

क्या रोयें हम ज़ार−ज़ार

क्योंकि यही है ज़िंदगी,

बस यही है ज़िंदगी.....

"किसके आने की उम्मीद ने दिल पर दस्तक दी,
किसकी सांसों की महक से सबा बहकी,
किसके कदमों की आहट से दिल की धड़कन मचली,
क्या यह वही मुसाफिर है जिसके इंतज़ार में रात तड़पी"

अनोखी शाम

दिन ढला, शाम के सुरमयी रंग निखरे,

हवा में घुल गयीं, गज़ब की शोखियां,

चांद खिला और फिज़ां में निखरी रंगीन मस्तियां,

ऐसे में जाने मन, जाने का नाम न लो,

दो पल की ज़िंदगी को एक ऐसी शाम दो,

जो मिट न सके ज़हन से मरते दम तक,

गुलों सी नर्म और खूबसूरत शाम को महका दो इतना,

कि, ताजा रहे यह खुशबू कयामत तक,

यह जहाँ जो मेरा है, तुम्हारे साथ है,

ये जो वक्त ठहरा है हमारे पास,

इस पल को जाने तमन्ना एक ज़िंदगी दे दो.....

मसल न जायें, तमन्नायें, रह न जाये अनबुझ प्यास,

कभी फुर्सत से करना जाने मन,

इन हसीन गुनाहों का हिसाब.....

प्याला सामने है,

उसमें डूब जाने दो,

इस पल को जाया न करो,

इस पल को एक ज़िंदगी दे दो......

"आहटों के फरेब में पहलें बिछा दीं,
तमन्नाओं ने दस्तक दी, तो ख्वाबों को जगह दी,
कैसे गुलों दिन और कैसे रंगीन रातें,
इश्क की आरजू में हमने ज़िंदगी गंवा दी......"

"तुम्हारे यादों की सौगात, अपने दिल के करीब रखते हैं,
इस दिल के बुझते चिराग तुम्हारे खयालों से जले हैं....."

खामोशी

दो सांसों से जुड़ी रह गयी यह ज़िंदगी,
गुज़र रही है कितनी खामोशी से,
न किसी तूफान की गुंजाइश,
न ख्वाबों का बसेरा,
छाया है चारों तरफ घनघोर अंधेरा,
ज़िंदगी कैद हुई उम्र के जाल में,
तड़पे जैसे मछली सूखे हुए तालाब में.....

"किस्मत की कैद में यह ज़िंदगी,
हाथ की लकीरों के ठिकाने पूछती हैं,
कैसे नादान है यह इंसान,
जो बेवफा ज़िंदगी से सहारे ढूंढती है....."

"ऐ गमें दिल थोड़ा और तड़प
ताकि ज़िंदा होने का एहसास रहे,
न तसव्वर हो उनका, न इश्की की इनायतें,
दर्दो गम का यह सिलसिला यूं ही चलता रहे....."

फना

जिनकी खुशी बनकर हम ज़मीं पर आते हैं,

वह वक्त में क्यों खो जाते हैं,

जो हमारी राहों को रौशन करते हैं,

जिनके नक्शे कदम पर, अपने नक्शे कदम बनाते हैं,

वह इस तरह फना क्यों हो जाते हैं,

जिनके साये में ज़िंदगी पनपी,

जिनके चेहरों से हमें रौशनी मिली,

वह सूरज की तरह क्यों ढल जाते हैं,

कल हम भी उन्हीं राहों पर चले जायेंगे,

हमारे भी नक्श–निशान यूं ही मिट जायेंगे,

आज के बच्चे फिर यही सवाल उठायेंगे,

कहाँ खो गये, कैसे गुम हो गये,

ज़िंदगी से मुंह मोड़कर क्यों चले गये,

लेकिन जवाब कहाँ से पायेंगे.....

"दूर कहीं पहाड़ियों के पीछे डूबता सूरज,
चहकते पंछियों का पेड़ों पर बसर,
नन्हें बच्चों पर मां की लोरियाँ का असर,
और मेरे ख्यालों में तुम्हारे ख्वाबों की डगर.....”

पाज़ेब....

आज सुबह—सुबह,

मेरी पाज़ेब से मधुर संगीत निकला,

कुछ पुरानी और कुछ नई यादें उभरीं,

मैं मस्त होकर सुनती रही,

एक—एक घुंघरू बजा,

हर एक राज़ खुला,

सदियों से जिन्हें सहेज रखा था,

आज तो गज़ब ही हो गया,

यह राग बुलंद होता गया,

और दिल, सहम कर रह गया,

किस—किस ने सुना और क्या सोचा,

कोई फिक्र नहीं,

मैं आंखें मूंदे चुपचाप पड़ी सुनती रही.....

तमाम खूबसूरत यादें जेहन से गुज़रीं,

यह मेहंदी रचे पांव पर खिला चमन,

यह पांव का आलिंगन बंधन, और बिछुए की चुभन,

इस सुखद घड़ी का अभिनंदन करता मेरा मन,

कितना सुंदर सपना था,

या एक सुहाना सच,

आज का दिन तो रस में डूब गया,

और मीठा हो गया, बहुत मीठा .....

"गनीमत है कि हम सुनते हैं, सिर्फ, कुछ कहते नहीं,
वरना जुबां के तीर कितनों को घायल कर देते हैं..."

"शुक्र करो कि हम गम सहते हैं, कहते नहीं,
वरना आंसुओं के सैलाब बह जाते और आप उसमें डूब जाते"

महक

वह सहमे कदमों का आगाज़,

जैसे खुशबू भरी हवा का झोंका,

वह नाज़ुक लबों का यूं खुलना,

जैसे पंखड़ियों का गुलाब से झड़ना,

वह लबों में दबी मुस्कुराहट,

जैसे किसी राज़ को छुपा रखना,

न शिकवे, न बातें, न कोई हिदायत

उन्हें आता है सब कुछ आंखों से बयां करना.....

"एक तन्हा मुसाफिर हूँ,
भटक गया गम की सूनी गलियों में,
कैसे ख्वाब, कैसी उम्मीदें,
आसरा ढूंढ रहा हूँ खाक में दफन होने को....."

"किस मोड़ पर आकर ठहरी है ज़िंदगी,
हसरतों का खात्मा, ख्वाहिशें को जुदा होते देखा,
न नये दर्द मिले, न अफसाने बने,
एक खामोश स्याह अंधेरे को डेरा डालते देखा......"

पुकार

खामोश आवाज़ों की पुकार,
सुनने वालों की तरसें,
खामोश माहौल की सदायें,
किसी दिल से टकराने को तरसें,
कैसा दर्द, कैसी फरियादें,
सब तो खामोशी में हैं कैद,
किसी खामोश इनसान को,
खामोशी तोड़ने को तरसे.....

"टूटे तारों को जोड़कर कुछ सुर निकले,
गमों को सुरों में डालकर कुछ गीत बने,
कोई सुने या न सुने उन्हें, कोई फिक्र नहीं,
हम तो इनसे अपना दिल बहला लेते हैं......"

"दिल के टूटे खंडहरों में भटकती यादें बार–बार पूछतीं,
कहाँ दब गयी वह सुकून की आहटें,
हमारी तुम्हारी गर्म सांसों की राहतें,
खामोश फिज़ां में खामोशी से फरियाद करती हैं,
फिर खामोशी से वक्त में दफन हो जाती हैं....."

वक्त

वक्त आहिस्ता–आहिस्ता, हाथों से सरक गया,
कब उतर गया गुलाबी शामों का नशा,
वह फूलों सी जगजमाती रातों का समा,
चांद कब छुप गया, पता भी न चला,
सुबह जब हुई, तो नशा उतर चुका था,

वक्त कैसे मुकाम पर छोड़ गया,
जहाँ सियाह आंखें और सूनी रातें,
न खयालों के तूफान, न ख्वाबों के हौसले,
न जिस्म में तपन, न रूह में प्यास,
सिर्फ एक भयानक खामोशी का एहसास,

खुशियों के कारवां आगे निकल गये,
क्यों इस ज़िंदगी में तन्हा हो गये,
और इस सुनसान राह के मुसाफिर बन गये,
ज़िंदगी से हम सवाल बार–बार करते हैं,
वक्त हाथों से क्यों सरक गया.....

"रात की स्याही में कुछ ख्वाबों को जगह दो,
महकती रातों को चांदनी से सजा दो,
खामोश ज़िंदगी को कुछ अरमानें की तमन्ना दो,
इस बेजान ज़िंदगी को धड़कनों की इजाज़त दो....."

"वक्त कहाँ से कहाँ गुजर गया,
वह पांव जो रूकते नहीं थे, कैसे थम गये,
ज़िंदगी का रस जैसे रिस–रिस कर निकल गया,
न तूफानी सांसों के कारवां, न रगों में तेज़ी,
ऐसी खामोशी छायी है, जैसे तूफान आकर गुज़र ग्रया....."

पहलू

वक्त कहाँ ठहरा है जैसा भी है गुज़र जाता है,

मौसम कब एक सा रहता है, बदल जाता है,

ज़िंदगी का सिलसिला यूं ही चलता जाता है,

हर सुबह महकती है नई उम्मीदों से,

हर शाम ढल जाती है अन्धेरों में

खुशियों के कारवां ठहरते हैं कुछ देर फिर आगे बढ़ जाते हैं,

यह दिल धड़ता रहता है कभी खुशी की इंतहा,

तो कभी गम की आंधियों से,

फिर थक कर एक दिन, धड़कना भूल जाता है।

"जमीं में दबे पत्थर हीरे बनकर चमकते हैं,
गर्दिश में दबे इंसान भी कुछ ऐसे ही निखरते हैं,
खुद का साथ, खुद की हिम्मत हो तो,
इंसान क्या कुछ नहीं कर सकते....."

"कहाँ वह फुरसतें, जो बनाये आशियानें,
कहाँ वह हसरतें, जो दिल जलायें आतिशें,
थम गये पाँव, थक गया बदन
आगे निकल गये कारवाँ सारे"

उम्मीद

बड़ी उम्मीद से हम आये इस ज़मीं पर,
बड़ी बेरूखी से रूख्सत हो जायेंगे एक दिन,
जिस बसेरे को गुलशन बनाया हमने,
उसे वीरान बनाकर चले जायेंगे,

कैसे आंखों ने देखे सुनहरे धोखे,
कैसी ख्वाबों में बनायी बुनियादें,
रेत के महल हैं यह,
हवा के झोखों से बिखर जायेंगे,

करूं किस से शिकवा, कहाँ आता है वो नज़र,
धोखे में रख सब को, ऐसा ढोंग रचाया उसने,
वह ज़िंदगी तो देता है खुदा बनकर,
और वापिस ले लेता है कातिल की तरह.....

"ज़िंदगी की तन्ह गहराइयों में,
तमाम दबी यादों को ढूंढ लेते हैं,
और पलकें मूंद कर तुम्हारी तस्वीर खींच लेते हैं...."

"गम की आतिश में जो चेहरा उभरा,?
उसकी रौशनी में दिल को जलाया,
मुझे छोड़कर जाने वाले,
फिर तेर रह गुज़र याद आया....."

मां

आज मंदिर की सीढ़ियों पर,
तुम्हारे पांव के निशान देखे,
आरती के दिये में तुम्हारा दमकता चेहरा,
उज्ज्वल, सौम्य, ममता रस बरसाता,

आज मंदिर के फूलों में तुम्हारी सुगंध महकी,
जब तुम नहाकर पूजा घर से निकलती,
सारा घर अपनी खुशबू में भर देती,
यह सुगंध मेरे मन की गहरायी में बसी है,

आज तुम्हारी यादों को रौशन करने,
मंदिर में एक दीप जलाया,
तुम्हारे कोमल हाथों का सुखद स्पर्श याद आया,
और तुम्हारे पवित्र प्यार को फिर मन में जगाया,

आज फिर कानों में घंटे आवाज़ गूंजी,
जो तुम मंदिर में बजाया करती,
आज अपने अस्तित्व को फिर तुमसे जुड़ा पाया,
और तुम्हारा जीवन दान याद आया.....

"खो गये ज़िंदगी के सहारे,
कहाँ जीने का सबब ढूंढें,
दिल तो गमों में कैद है,
कैसे इसकी रिहायी ढूंढे....."

"तन्हाई के अंधेरों में सहमे हुए गम,
फिरते रहे काले सायों की तरह,
तुम आये दिल का करार बनकर,
स्याह बादलों को चीर, रोशनी की किरण बनकर....."

आह.....

जिंदगी एक आह बनकर रह गयी,
दर्द की कराहटों की राह बनकर रह गई'',
झड़ गये फूल सब्ज शाखों से,
एक सूखी डाल बनकर रह गयी,

ढल गयी वह शबनमी रातें,
दब गया रंग गुलों का,
उड़ गयी खुशबू हवाओं से,
सिर्फ उन यादों की फिज़ां बनकर रह गयी,

तरस रही है वीरान ज़िंदगी,
कुछ शबनमी रातों को,
ओस की बूंद की नमी,
गर्मी महकती सांसों की,

अब भी कुछ शोलों में गर्मी बाकी है,
कुछ अनसुने नगमों की गूंज, कुछ ख्वाबों की बुनियाद,
ज़रा इस राह पर पेशे कदमों से गुज़र कर तो देखो,
दिल में कुछ धड़कनें अभी बाकी हैं.....

"होंठों की फीकी मुस्कुराहट में बसी आहें,
सिसकियों की मन्नत मांगे,
आंखों की अधूरी नींदें,
ख्वाबों के सहारे भागे......"

गम

जब गम ने पनाह ली,

तमाम दर्द ज़हन में उभरे,

भूली बिसरी यादों के हुजूम,

बेतकल्लुफ तशरीफ़ लाये,

बिन बुलाये मेहमान जैसे,

दिल में अपने नक्शे कदम जमाये,

लाख समझाया कि आगे बढ़ो,

कोई और घर ढूंढ़ो, दफा हो यहाँ से,

नहीं सुना, ढीठ मन ने,

बहुत तड़पाया ज़ालिम ने,

दिल को दर्द में डुबोया,

आंसू बन रिस–रिस के निकला,

कमबख़्त चूर–चूर कर गया.....

"कभी खयालों में, कभी ख्वाबों में,
वह आता है मेरे होश उड़ाने को,
न दिखता है, न मिलता है,
छोड़ जाता है दिल पर कदमों के निशानें को......"

कर्ज़

कर्ज़ में मिली है ज़िंदगी,

कायम रहेगी आखिर कब तक,

कर ले कुछ नेकियां, लूट ले चंद खुशियां,

ज़ाया न कर, नेमत से मिली इस दौलत को,

बस थोड़ी मोहलत बक्शी है जीने की,

जाने कब दावते मौत की दस्तक आ जाये,

लोग एहतियात से जीते हैं, मानो सदियों का बसेरा हो,

लेकिन वक्त कब ठहरा और ज़िंदगी कब रुकी,

मिल ले ज़िंदगी से ज़रा ज़िंदा दिली से,

कयामत में दर्ज़ होने से पहले,

क्योंकि कर्ज़ में मिली है यह ज़िंदगी,

कायम रहेगी कब तक....

"बड़ी बेदर्दी से वह इस दिल को तोड़कर चले गये,
पर उनकी रहम दिली को देखो,
जाते–जाते एक सुपर–ग्लू की बोतल छोड़ गये....."

तूफान

ज़िंदगी गुज़र रही थी, गुज़र जाती,

वक्त गुज़र रहा था, गुज़र जाता,

लेकिन इसमें एक तूफान को आना था,

कितनी खामोशी से जी रहे थे हम,

इसमें आग का दरिया लाना था,

न बिजली चमकी, न आंधी चली,

उसके गुलो कदमों की आहट को एक हंगामा मचाना था,

इन बेवफा आंखों ने देखा उसे, इन्हीं से धोखा हमें खाना था,

न ये नज़रें मिलती, न दिल पर छुरियां चलती,

उसे तो मेरे ही दिल में, अपना ठिकाना बनाना था.....

"तेरी खुशी की इंतिहा में ऐसे मशगूल हुए सनम,
कि खुद को, खुद से, जुदा कर दिया....."

एक शाम

एक खूबसूरत शाम,

सिर्फ तुम्हारे नाम,

तुम्हारी मुस्कुराहट, तुम्हारी आंखों की चमक,

और तमाम बीती यादों की महक,

सब का बनकर जाम, होंठों से लगाया है,

और बिस्तर पर ख्वाबों को सजाया है....

पल भर को बंद आंखों में हुआ है तुम्हारे होने का एहसास,

तुम्हारे बदन की खुशबू, तुम्हारी जुल्फों का आभास,

तुम्हारे बदन के शोले फिर आग भड़का देते हैं,

और तमाम हसरतों को वाबस्ता जवां कर देते हैं....

बस आंख बंद कर तुम्हें महसूस करता रहूं,

और खुदा से मिलने की मन्नत मांगता रहूं,

तुम रूखसत हुए, जुदा हुई, तमन्नायें

रह गयीं गुलशन में खामोश और मायूस सदायें.....

इस शाम की निखरी यादों के सहारे,

उनमें डूबकर रह जाना है,

तुम्हारी मुस्कुराहट और आंखों की चमक,

मेरी सांसों में, तुम्हारी सांसों की महक,

इनका जाम बनाकर पीना, और कुछ पल जीना है....

"दो लम्हे साथ क्या गुज़ारे,
तुम तो मेरे दिल में ही उतर गये,
आंखों के झरोखों में जगह दी,
जो ज़िंदगी भर के मेहमान बन गये....."

न जाने क्यों....

बारिश के पानी में डूबती, कागज़ की कशती,

बागों में झड़ती फूलों की पंखुड़ियां,

क्यों दिल के अरमान तोड़ती हैं,

बादल में छुपे चांद से क्यों ज़िंदगी अधूरी सी लगती है,

ठंडी बरसाती हवायें क्यों अकेले पन का एहसास देती हैं,

नन्हे बच्चे की हंसी, क्यों दिल को भीतर तक छू जाती है,

ये कैसे सवालात हैं, कहाँ ढून्डें इनके जवाब,

यूं ही बार—बार मेरे ज़हन में

अक्सर ख्यालात आ जाते हैं....

"गम के दरिया हैं कैद इन आंखों में,
ऐ आंसुओं इन्हें रिहायी दे दो,
कुछ गम कम हों ज़िंदगी के,
तो नये गमों की गुंजाइश होगी....."

बिदाई....

बाबुल के घर से रूख्सत हुई,
पांव में हज़ार कांटों की चुभन लिये,
नये गुलशन में आशियाँ बनाने,
तमाम यादों को आंचल में लपेटे,
आंखों में आंसुओं के सैलाब लिये,
सांसों में जज्बों के तूफान समेटे,
ममता की चादर ओढ़े मां, गुमसुम सी खड़ी,
तमाम आंसू ढलकाती सोच रही,
कहाँ खो गयी वह नन्ही परी,
जो घर आंगन में खुशियाँ बिखराती,
पिता पत्थर की मीनार बने,
सीने में दर्द छिपाये सोच रहे थे
आंगन में पली ये नाजुक कली,
सारी खशबू बटोर कर चली,
सूना हो जायेगा गुलिस्तां मेरा,
सूनी हो जायेगी ये ज़िंदगी मेरी.....

खुदा महफूज रख्खे

वह हाथ जो इबादत के लिये उठते हैं,
वह हाथ जिनसे मंदिर में दीपक जलते हैं,
वह हाथ जो आशीर्वाद में उठते हैं,
खुदा उन्हें महफूज रखे.....

वह पांव जो घर की दहलीज को, चमन का आगाज़ बनाते हैं,
वह पांव जो मंदिरों में पूजे जाते हैं,
वह पांव जिनकी आहट से दिल के दरवाज़े खुल जाते हैं,
खुदा उन्हें महफूज रखे....

वह ममता भरी बाहें, जिनमें नन्हें फरिश्ते पलते हैं,
वह बाहें जिनमें आपके दुःख दर्द मिट जाते हैं,?
वह बाहें जिनसे जन्मों के रिश्ते जुड़ते हैं,
खुदा उन्हें महफूज रखे....

वह आंखे जो आपकी राह में पलकें बिछाती हैं,
वह आंखें जो आपके दुःख दर्द में बह जाती हैं,
वह आंखे जो ममता के मोती बिखराती हैं,
खुदा उन्हें महफूज रखे....

"वह लब जो गाकर, चांद सितारों को सुला देते हैं,
वह लब जो शोख़ी से मुस्करा देते हैं,
वह लब जो मुस्करा कर फूलों को शरमा देते हैं,
खुदा उन्हें महफूज रखे...."

"वह ममता से छलकता दिल,
वह सब के रंज–ओ–गम में दुखता दिल,
वह आपके लिये धड़कता दिल,
खुदा उसे महफूज रखे...."

"मेरे तन्हा ज़िंदगी के हमसफर,
ख्यालों में देखा, ख्वाबों में तुम्हें सजाया,
दिल ने तुम्हें आवाज़ दी, और धड़कनों में बसाया,
काली स्याह रातों का सहारा बनकर,
बरसात की रिमझिम में तुम्हें गुनगुनाया...."

कंगन....

आज फिर तुम्हारे कंगन से भूली बिसरी यादें निखरीं,

कुछ शबनमी रातों के जज़्बे,

कुछ गर्म सांसों के नगमें,

कजरारी आंखों में डूबी रातें,

माथे पर भटकी आवारा ज़ुल्फें,

तुम्हें संवारतीं, और निखारतीं,

फूलों की खशबू सी सजी से पर तुम,

जवां ज़िंदगी की एक गज़ल बन जातीं.....

चलते फिरते तुम यूं ही मिल गये थे,
जैसे सदियों से तुम्हें जाना हो,
लेकिन जुदा हुए तुम ऐसे,
जैसे इस ज़िंदगी में तुम्हारा आना ही न था....

कभी

कभी हम भी गुलशन-ए-बहार थे,

हसरतों के चमन गुलज़ार थे,

कुछ हमारा भी रूतबा था,

उनकी धड़कनों में हमारा बसेरा था,

उनके दिल का हम करार थे,

इस दिल में इश्क का रंग था,

ज़िंदगी में खुशियों का मजमा था,

क्या वक्त था, क्या इश्क था,

वक्त ने बगावत की हमसे,

उम्र के कांटों को चुभना था,

वह वक्त गया, दिल तन्हा हुआ.....

महसूस

ख्यालों में देखा, ख्वाबों में सजाया,
दिल ने तुम्हें आवाज़ दी और धड़कनों में बसाया,
काली स्याह रातों में सहारा बनाकर
बरसात की रिमझिम में तुम्हें गुनगुनाया,
मेरी तन्हा ज़िंदगी के हमसफर,
मेरे खयालों के चराग, रौशनी ज़िंदगी की कहाँ हो तुम,
मेरी कशिश महसूस करो और चले जाओ.....

www.ingramcontent.com/pod-product-compliance
Lightning Source LLC
LaVergne TN
LVHW051535170726

843492LV00006B/1782